Trust in
the
Lord and
Lady
to guide
your workings.

M.W. Russell

DOWN THE WITCHES' WAY

by

M.W. ROMAN

for
Lady
Luna

foreword

This book is to be considered a primer for all those who seek magic, for the inquisitive, the spiritual explorers and for the brave. Presented here are the basics of sorcery, a foundation from which to build your own witchcraft.

Belief
is the
Key

Introduction

Invisible forces shape our world, whether it be the change in the seasons, the moon's effect upon the seas or the chemistry between two people. To work magic is to understand these forces and bend them to your will. However, the most important step along this path is to BELIEVE. Have faith in your connection to nature and learn to use it.

Witchcraft is not just a set of skills, it is also a belief system and perhaps the oldest form of religion. There is a God as well as a Goddess, a code of conduct, and it requires unwavering faith. We celebrate the ancient holidays, called Sabbats, on the ever turning wheel.

SABBATS

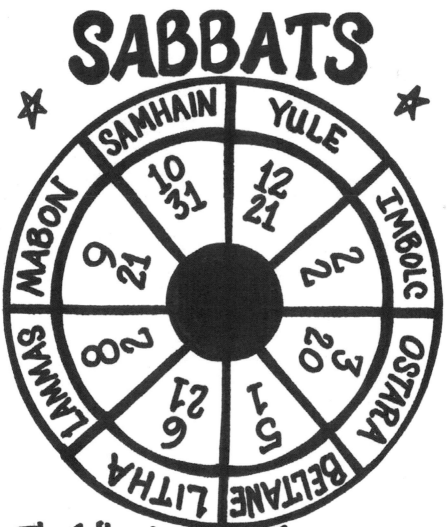

The Wheel of the Year contains
the holidays of Old, each of which
a story to be told.

SAMHAIN

Long is the Night
Long are the shadows
The Dead will rise
On the Eve of All Hallows

Samhain is the start
of winter and marks
the Witches' New Year,
a time when the veil
between the living and
the dead is thinnest.
Honor those who've passed
and you may consult them.

Yule

Burning candles on the bough
Alight the sacrificial sow
Divine upon an icy pool
On the night that we call Yule

Yule is the Winter Solstice, the longest night of the year. It is a celebration of the light returning from the darkness, of rebirth and of hope. Celebrate with gifts.

Light a white candle
and place it in the window
to make sure the Sun
comes again tomorrow

Imbolc marks the start of Spring and is a fire festival about purification and renewal. Lighting candles symbolizes the increasing power of the sun and its warmth.

o

Ostara is the Spring equinox, a celebration of fertility and regeneration as the earth recovers from the cold of Winter. Outdoor activities return as the World blooms once again.

BELTANE

Dance around the pole
to usher in the summer
the young and the old
may each take a lover

Beltane is the beginning of Summer, when livestock are driven out again to feed in green pastures. Activities include dancing around the May Pole, frolicking and bonfires.

The longest day with the Sun so high marks the change when the Dark draws nigh

Litha is Midsummer. A time for celebrating and rejoicing and correcting negative aspects of our lives. This holiday is marked by carnivals and fairs and fireworks.

LAMMAS

Take the sickle to the stock
to bake the first bread and
make sure the Goddess
is properly fed.

Lammas is the start of Autumn and the first harvest. The weather is still very warm, but the leaves begin to brown. Bread is baked and eaten in celebration of the Gods and nature's bounty.

o

MABON

Now has come the time
for rest for arts and
crafts and warmer dress

Mabon, the Autumn equinox and second harvest. This is the time when darkness overtakes the light. The contemplation of mysteries and personal reflection are appropriate.

May the
Lord and
Lady bless
your workings

The horned God is ☆
connected to the Sun
and forests, has many
earthly associations and
is known as the Green Man
☾ ○ ☽

The Goddess has a triple
aspect of Maiden,
Mother and Crone in
connection with the
phases of the moon and
is known as Lady Luna

Secrecy

Keep your work between you and the Gods. Do not share that which you seek lest the negativity of others weaken it.

Although over 300 years have passed since the dark Trials, we still live in ignorant times. For this reason you may choose to keep your practice secret.

Silentium est Aureum

<u>Please Note</u>

Contained within these
pages is but one way,
when in fact there are
many different paths
that may lead you
Down the Witches' Way.

The Elements

Earth
Abundance, Wealth
prosperity and stability.
North

Water
Emotions, love
purification and
the subconscious.
West

Air
Intelligence,
psychic power
and dreams.
East

Fire
Energy, passion
inspiration and leadership.
South

☽ Moon
♂ Mars
☿ Mercury
♃ Jupiter
♀ Venus
♄ Saturn
☉ Sun

▽ Earth
△ AIR
△ FIRE
▽ WATER

SYMBOLS

The Pentacle

The five-pointed star is
a symbol of the old
religion and is used for
power and protection.

Drawing the Star
without a circle is
called the pentagram.

for
banishing

for
invoking

Drawn onto paper,
in the air or on a candle
the pentagram is potent.

ASTROLOGY

ARIES
3/19 - 4/18

TAURUS
4/19 - 5/19

GEMINI
5/20 - 6/19

CANCER
6/20 - 7/21

LEO
7/22 - 8/21

VIRGO
8/22 - 9/21

LIBRA
9/22 - 10/21

SCORPIO
10/22 - 11/20

SAGITARIUS
11/21 - 12/20

CAPRICORN
12/21 - 1/19

AQUARIUS
1/20 - 2/17

PISCES
2/18 - 3/18

💀 The Dead 💀

Energy cannot be destroyed, it can only take on a different form. Therefore Death is not the end, but a new beginning. Fear not and call upon them.

Sound Familiar?

A familiar is an animal that is extra special to witchcraft as they can strengthen your spells.

Oftentimes it is the familiar who chooses the witch. Care for them.

☆ ☆ ☆ ☆ ☆ ☆

Witchcraft is a skill as well as a religion. It requires both practice and faith for mastery.

☆ ☆

TOOLS
of the trade →

☆

BELL
Symbol of the Goddess

Used to ring out our intention, to invoke or to banish

BOOK

The power of the written word and repository of knowledge

CANDLE

Symbol of divine light that burns within and powers our spells

CUP
Symbol of the Goddess used for ceremonial offerings and drink

CAULDRON
Cast iron and three-legged used for burning & boiling

ATHAME
Symbol of the God ceremonial blade used for casting and cutting

Broom

Also known as a besom, the broom is an essential tool used for cleansing ritual space, to purify and to protect and to sweep away any negative energy.

Body

Your body is your most important tool and should be treated as such. Take care of your body with healthy foods, exercise and plenty of rest. Drink water often and red wine for special occasions. Do not be ashamed of your body for you will only have one.

Cleanse your tools before using in the smoke of a burning sage stick

Consecrate your tools next with earth, air, fire and water

Charge your tools over night in the light of the full moon

Gather your Tools ✸
All Witches and fools
Under the light of the Moon
Head to the brambles
Away from the shambles ✸
Under the light of the Moon
✸ Your darkest desire
To cast on the fire
Under the light of the Moon
With flora and fauna
And fresh belladonna ✸
Dancing and Chanting
And Casting our Spells
Under the light of the Moon

Have you ever wondered ⑦
why we have 7 days
in a week?

Monday ~ Lunes ~ Moon
Tuesday ~ Martes ~ Mars
Wednesday ~ Miercoles ~ Mercury
Thursday ~ Jueves ~ Jupiter
Friday ~ Viernes ~ Venus
Saturday ~ Sabado ~ Saturn
Sunday ~ Domingo ~ Sun
⑦ · · · · · · · · · ⑦

the 7 Celestial Bodies of the Ancient World

☆ ☆ ☆

Moon ~ women, dreams, intuition

Mars ~ aggression, sex, male

Mercury ~ communication, wisdom

Jupiter ~ travel, wealth

Venus ~ beauty, love, art

Saturn ~ reality, laws, tests

Sun ~ creativity, health

Make good use of the
days of the week to fortify
that which you seek

☆ ((O)) ☆

Pray to the Moon when she
is round and luck for you
shall then abound and
what you seek for shall
be found in sea or sky
or on solid ground

• • • • •

Magic can be done anywhere and anytime and as simply or as thorough as you like, but the use of **Ritual** will help to clearly set your intentions and strengthen your Witchcraft.

☆

Anoint

Dab some blessing oils on your pulse points and inhale their scent deeply.

Meditate

Sit comfortably and close your eyes. Breathe deeply and slowly and clear your mind.

Cast the Circle

North, Earth, Green

SACRED

SPACE

West, Water, Blue

East, Air, Yellow

South, Fire, Red

Inside the circle you are in that time that is not a time and that place that is not a place - the center of the universe. You are _protected_ and _empowered_. Sweep clockwise to cleanse and cast clockwise with Athame.

Call the Quarters

Start in the North and move clockwise through the East, South and West.

say...

"Hail to the Guardians of the Watchtower of the _North_, element of _Earth_. I ask that you please join me in my magic circle tonight."

then...

Light a _green_ candle.

Etc.

Invoke the Gods

"I humbly ask that the Lord and Lady bless this circle with their presence and divine wisdom."

Light the White candle.

NOW...

RENOUNCE

YOUR OLD BELIEFS.
CAST AWAY ALL OF
YOUR OLD NOTIONS
ABOUT HOW THE
WORLD WORKS AND
WHAT YOUR PLACE IS
WITHIN IT. PRICK YOUR
FINGER TO DRAW BLOOD
AND <u>DEDICATE</u> <u>YOURSELF</u>.

As Above So Below

We are a microcosm of the Universe, made up of billions of atoms that are like the stars.

Therefore, to make change in the world, I must seek to change myself. I am as the universe.

When
    finished...
with ritual, or even
simple spellcasting,
it is essential as
well as polite to
thank and release
all those who you
have "invited". Then
release your circle by
moving widdershins.

WONDER

Curiosity will be
the fuel that drives
all of your creativity

INTENT

Spellcasting requires little more than the will to manifest your dreams and desires

RESPECT

Only with a genuine regard for nature will you be able to harness her power

CALM

You must learn
to quiet your mind
and relax in order
to focus your magic

Divination

To seek knowledge of the future or that which is hidden. To gaze into a reflective surface, to toss the bones or to consult the cards — all of which are old forms of divination meant to help you in your spells or to guide others who seek your counsel. The most infamous of these is the TAROT.

------>

Simple Tarot

These cards are like the regular plaging cards we all know, but with a special additional set of 22 that tell a universal tale of the fool's Journey. We all play the fool at one time in our lives, and we also can be teachers, students, Kings and Queens.

So... Let's keep it simple.

The 22 Major Arcana cards tell the Fool's Journey

The 56 Minor Arcana cards are comprised of four Suits

earth **Pentacles** – Wealth

air **Swords** – Intellect

fire **Wands** – Passion

water **Cups** – Love

The Major Cards

0. Fool – Unknown
1. Magician – will
2. Priestess – intuition
3. Empress – mother
4. Emperor – father
5. Hierophant – ritual
6. Lovers – union
7. Chariot – travel
8. Strength – spirit
9. Hermit – teacher
10. Wheel – cycles

11. Justice – legality
12. Hanged – divination
13. Death – change
14. Temperance – mixing
15. Devil – weakness
16. Tower – turmoil
17. Star – wishes
18. Moon – dreams
19. Sun – happiness
20. Judgement – calling
21. World – reward

The Minor Cards

Ace begin/end

2. dualism/pair

3. trinity

4. stability

5. loss, Sadness

6. harmony

7. Conflict

8. mature balance

9. near the limit

10. maximum

Page - youth

Knight-defender

Queen - Motherly

King - Commander

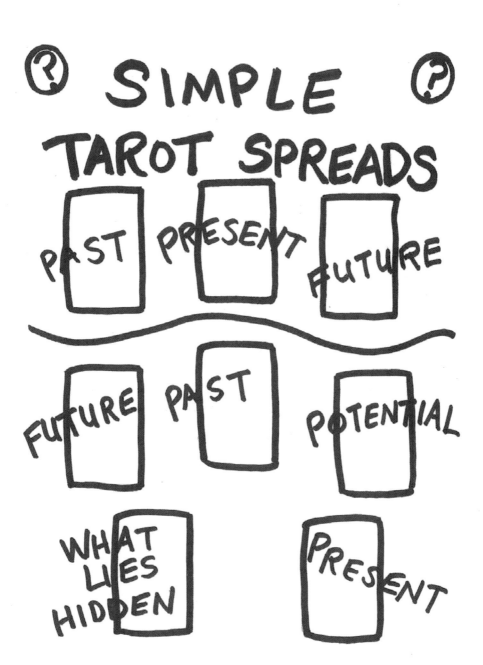

READ THE
TAROT

for yourself
for friends
for spells

∘
∘
∘

Often

★

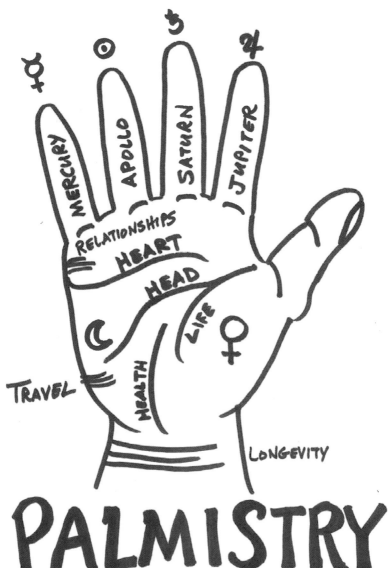

PALMISTRY

Candle Magic

The use of candles is common in all forms of Spirituality. In witchcraft it is not passive, as in prayer, but active, and relies upon intention.

Burn your candles
to bring something
to you, to take something
away, to talk to the
dead or commune
with your Gods, but
burn them with care,
always beware.

Purposeful intention
combined with proper
color correspondence
is made even more
powerful on the
right day of the
week.

Black: binding, removing

White • purity, peace

Green • earth, healing

Yellow • air, intellect

Red • fire, passion

Blue • water, love

-¢- ~ -¢- ~ -¢-

Silver • the Goddess, dreams

Gold • the God, happiness

Purple • psychic, occult

Pink • affection, romance

Brown • favors, friends

Orange • success, legality

-φ- ~ -φ- ~ -φ-

Candles can be inscribed with symbols or names, annointed with various oils or combined for specific purposes. The flame glows, flickers and eventually burns out, just as we will.

Sigils

A very simple, yet highly effective form of magic that is powered by the use of symbols that may be eaten or carried, burned or burried.

Bones of the Dead

Place this sigil under your pillow on a Monday to dream of the dead.

Courageous Sun

Draw on a Tuesday
morning and keep in
pocket throughout week

The Ninth Gate

Draw in chalk under
the front doormat on
a Wednesday to open a
gateway of communication

Jupiter's Bank

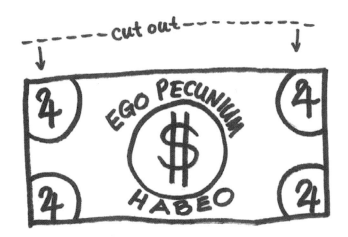

Draw and place in your wallet on a Thursday to bring wealth into your life

The Great Bond of Love

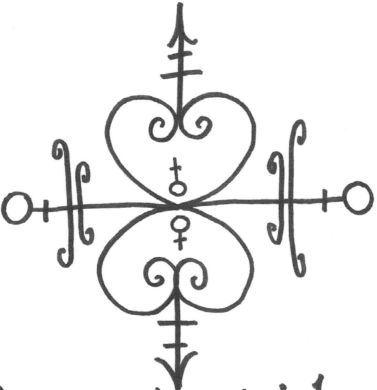

Draw on toast in honey
and share with lover
on Friday morning

Hand of Glory

ᛏ   ᛏ

I bind   (nomen).

ᛏ   ᛏ

Burn on a Saturday
to bind those who
seek to do you harm.

The Winged Star

Draw and then burn
this sigil on a Sunday
and place ashes in
the shoes of loved one

Sigils Made of Words

1) <u>State your Intention</u>

I WILL LOSE
FIVE POUNDS

2) <u>Remove the Vowels</u>

I W~~I~~LL L~~O~~S~~E~~
F~~I~~V~~E~~ P~~O~~~~U~~NDS

3) <u>Remove repeating Letters</u>

W L S F V P N D

4) <u>Combine into Sigil</u>

✦ ☆

5) <u>Charge and Burn Sigil</u>

At this point you
are ready to work
your magic

Spells

Warning

Do not enter the craft of spellcasting lightly. Be careful of that which you do and mindful of what you say. Spells are much more powerful than words alone. ⊗

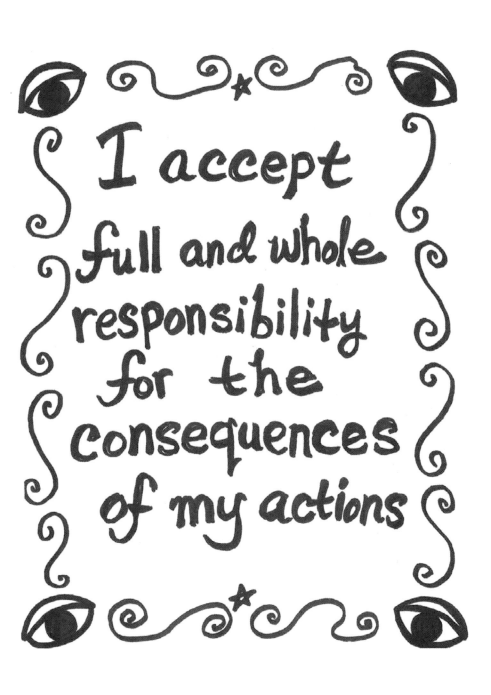

☆ for the NEW MOON ☆

Tonight marks a New Me
a new Me on the New Moon
a new Me I will see very soon
Tonight marks a new beginning
a new beginning on the New Moon
a new beginning I will see very soon
Tonight marks a fresh start
a fresh start on the New Moon
a fresh start I will see very soon
I am happy - I am healthy
I am blessed - I am loved.

New Moon
Manifestation

Sit still and relax.
Think of all the things
you are thankful for.
Write down what you want
to manifest, beginning
with the phrase "I am,"
or "I have." Save your list
until the full moon and
then burn it, releasing
your magical intentions.

The Witches' Bottle

This spell is to be done while the moon is waxing

1) Clean out an old bottle

2) Add a pinch of sea salt and some blessing oil

3) Write down your wish, roll it up and place in bottle

4) Cover cork in white wax and tie bottle neck with white cord

5) Hang from tree or bury in the yard

Burnt Offerings

Spell works best when the
Moon is waxing or full —
To give thanks to your Gods
for all your many blessings

1) Light a fire outdoors
2) Write down three things
   you are most thankful for
3) Fold the paper three times
   and kiss the paper three x
4) Drop onto the flames and
   watch as your words burn

The Jabber Jar

Spell only works when the moon is on the wane and is meant to banish or release

1) Fill an old jar with banishing herbs such as mugwort

2) Place the jar to your mouth and say the things you want to be rid of inside

3) Quickly tighten the lid, walk widdershins three x

4) Cover with a cloth and smash to release ⊕

The Three Leaves Spell

To hasten Spring or to bring
about change or renewal
1) Lay three dried leaves
   in a triangular pattern
   and light a green candle
   in the center and say...
"These three leaves, a gift
from the earth, Birth to Death
and Death to Birth. Change
the dark to light of day
Day to Night, Night to Day"

Coven Cord Ritual

To tighten the bond of witches within a coven

1) Coven members form a tight circle and relax.

2) Each witch ties the cord to their left wrist, moving in a clockwise fashion.

3) Members spit into each other's palms, clasp hands and raise their arms up...

"So Mote It Be"

The Purloin Poppet

Saturday – Waxing Moon

Take clothing from your adversary, fold it once and cut out a simple figure. Fill with garlic, mugwort, pepper and hair from brush. Sew into poppet and bind with black thread, saying...
"To be protected from you, I bind this poppet of you."

Thirteen Candles ☽

When the moon wanes, set up a circle of thirteen black candles, moving widdershins. Sit quietly and take thirteen deep breaths, concentrating on what you want to remove from your life. Extinguish candles in same fashion while saying intentions out loud!

To Remove Anxiety

Upon arrival at the Great Oak Tree, I bring greetings and Hail to thee. With hand outstretched in supplicant plea, I walk widdershins Three times Three. Oh Great Oak of Beauty and Power, take away the fears of my darkest hour, remove the shackles that Keep Me bound and I shall honor your hallowed ground."

Chant to Raise Energy

"Give me a Skin for dancing in
With Bone as hard as Stone
Take my Hand, We'll go around
Again and Again and Again
Let there be Lips for Kissing with
And a Cup for the Drinking
Let us Rejoice and raise our Voice
As One to the Lady Above"

"The Earth empowers our Magic
The Air empowers our Magic
Fire empowers our Magic
And Water empowers our Magic"

For the FULL MOON

Full Moon, fullest Moon
Hear these Words and Grant
this Boon - lend Me the
Key to your Secret Room
Where the Wisdom of
Years, Tarot and Rune is
Carried on a Breeze
Like a Whispering Tune

Ye Olde Good Luck CHARM BAG

5" x 5" piece of green cloth

1 moonstone
1 tiger's eye
1 acorn
fresh clover
pinch of thyme

Combine items into cloth and tie with white ribbon. Carry in pocket for luck.

Bright

✷

☽

Blessings

✷

Now you are ready to create your own spells and rituals. Use the contents of this book as a foundation from which to build upon.

~Notes~

_____

_____

_____

_____

_____

_____

~ Notes ~

_____

_____

_____

_____

_____

_____

~Notes~

_____

_____

_____

_____

_____

_____

~ Notes ~

_____

_____

_____

_____

_____

_____

~ Notes ~

_____

_____

_____

_____

_____

_____